Recipes to make ~~~~~~ gifts

Use these recipes to delight your friends and family. Each recipe includes gift tags for your convenience — just cut them out and personalize!

After personalizing your tag, fold and attach it to the top of the bag (above the sealed strip). Attach the tag with staples, or for a more decorative gift in a bag, use raffia, ribbon, twine, yarn or string. To do this, punch one or more holes in the top of your bag and tag at the same time. Then secure the tag using the raffia, ribbon, twine, yarn or string.

These gifts should keep for up to six months.

Printed in China

Distributed By:

CQProducts

507 Industrial Street
Waverly, IA 50677

ISBN 1-56383-140-6

Orange Hot Chocolate Mix

2 1/4 T. powdered coffee creamer
1 T. powdered orange flavored drink mix
1 1/2 T. powdered sugar
1 1/2 T. powdered chocolate flavored drink mix

Combine the above ingredients and stir until well blended. Place in a 3" x 4" ziplock bag and seal.

Attach a gift tag with the directions on how to prepare the hot chocolate.

Orange Hot Chocolate

To make one serving:
1 1/2 to 2 T. Orange Hot Chocolate Mix
8 ounces (1 cup) boiling water
Marshmallows or whipped cream, optional

Place the Orange Hot Chocolate Mix in a mug. Pour boiling water over the mixture. Stir until the mix is completely dissolved. If desired, garnish with marshmallows or whipped cream. Package of Orange Hot Chocolate Mix makes 5 to 8 servings.

Orange Hot Chocolate

To make one serving:
1 1/2 to 2 T. Orange Hot Chocolate Mix
8 ounces (1 cup) boiling water
Marshmallows or whipped cream, optional

Place the Orange Hot Chocolate Mix in a mug. Pour boiling water over the mixture. Stir until the mix is completely dissolved. If desired, garnish with marshmallows or whipped cream. Package of Orange Hot Chocolate Mix makes 5 to 8 servings.

The best gifts are tied
with heart strings.

fold

Orange Hot Chocolate

To make one serving:
1 1/2 to 2 T. Orange Hot Chocolate Mix
8 ounces (1 cup) boiling water
Marshmallows or whipped cream, optional

Place the Orange Hot Chocolate Mix in a mug. Pour boiling water over the mixture. Stir until the mix is completely dissolved. If desired, garnish with marshmallows or whipped cream. Package of Orange Hot Chocolate Mix makes 5 to 8 servings.

Laughter is the
sunlight of the soul.

- - - - - - - - - - fold - - - - - - - - - - - -

Hot Apple Cider Mix

2 T. presweetened lemonade mix
2 T. sugar
1 tsp. ground cinnamon
1/2 tsp. ground nutmeg

Combine the above ingredients and stir until well blended. Place in a 3" x 4" ziplock bag and seal.

Attach a gift tag with the directions on how to prepare the cider.

Hot Apple Cider

To make one serving:
1 tsp. Hot Apple Cider Mix
8 ounces (1 cup) hot apple juice
Cinnamon stick, optional

Place the Hot Apple Cider Mix in a mug. Pour hot apple juice over the mixture. Stir until the mix is completely dissolved. If desired, garnish with cinnamon stick. Package of Hot Apple Cider Mix makes 16 servings when added to 1 gallon of hot apple juice.

Hot Apple Cider

To make one serving:
1 tsp. Hot Apple Cider Mix
8 ounces (1 cup) hot apple juice
Cinnamon stick, optional

Place the Hot Apple Cider Mix in a mug. Pour hot apple juice over the mixture. Stir until the mix is completely dissolved. If desired, garnish with cinnamon stick. Package of Hot Apple Cider Mix makes 16 servings when added to 1 gallon of hot apple juice.

To handle yourself -- use your head.
To handle others -- use your heart.

-- -- -- -- -- -- -- -- -- -- fold -- -- -- -- -- -- --

Hot Apple Cider

To make one serving:
1 tsp. Hot Apple Cider Mix
8 ounces (1 cup) hot apple juice
Cinnamon stick, optional

Place the Hot Apple Cider Mix in a mug. Pour hot apple juice over the mixture. Stir until the mix is completely dissolved. If desired, garnish with cinnamon stick. Package of Hot Apple Cider Mix makes 16 servings when added to 1 gallon of hot apple juice.

Kindness, like a boomerang,
always returns.

‑ ‑ ‑ ‑ ‑ ‑ ‑ · fold‑ ‑ ‑ ‑ ‑ ‑ ‑ ‑ ‑

Swiss Mocha Mix

3 T. powdered instant dry milk
1 1/2 T. instant coffee granules
1 1/2 T. sugar
1/2 tsp. plus 1/8 tsp. unsweetened cocoa

Combine the above ingredients and stir until well blended. Place in a 3" x 4" ziplock bag and seal.

Attach gift tag with the directions on how to prepare the mocha.

Swiss Mocha

To make one serving:
2 to 2 1/2 tsp. Swiss Mocha Mix
8 ounces (1 cup) boiling water
Whipped cream, optional

Place Swiss Mocha Mix in a mug. Pour boiling water over the mixture. Stir until the mix is completely dissolved. If desired, garnish with whipped cream. Package of Swiss Mocha Mix makes 5 to 8 servings.

Swiss Mocha

To make one serving:
2 to 2 1/2 tsp. Swiss Mocha Mix
8 ounces (1 cup) boiling water
Whipped cream, optional

Place Swiss Mocha Mix in a mug. Pour boiling water over the mixture. Stir until the mix is completely dissolved. If desired, garnish with whipped cream. Package of Swiss Mocha Mix makes 5 to 8 servings.

Go forth into the busy world and love it. Interest yourself in life, mingle kindly with its joys and sorrows.

-Ralph Waldo Emerson

- - - - - - fold - - - - - - -

Swiss Mocha

To make one serving:
2 to 2 1/2 tsp. Swiss Mocha Mix
8 ounces (1 cup) boiling water
Whipped cream, optional

Place Swiss Mocha Mix in a mug. Pour boiling water over the mixture. Stir until the mix is completely dissolved. If desired, garnish with whipped cream. Package of Swiss Mocha Mix makes 5 to 3 servings.

It is a good thing to be rich,
and a good thing to be strong,
but it is a better thing to be loved
by many friends.

-Euripides

- - - - - - - - fold - - - - - - -

Toffee Coffee Mix

4 tsp. instant coffee granules
2 T. powdered coffee creamer
2 T. brown sugar

Combine the above ingredients and stir until well blended. Place in a 3" x 4" ziplock bag and seal.

Attach a gift tag with the directions on how to prepare the coffee.

❀ For a great gift, put three or four different hot drink mixes in a mug. ❀

Toffee Coffee

To make one serving:
2 to 3 tsp. Toffee Coffee Mix
8 ounces (1 cup) boiling water

Place the Toffee Coffee Mix in a mug. Pour boiling water over the mixture. Stir until the mix is completely dissolved. Package of Toffee Coffee Mix makes 5 to 8 servings.

Toffee Coffee

To make one serving:

2 to 3 tsp. Toffee Coffee Mix
8 ounces (1 cup) boiling water

Place the Toffee Coffee Mix in a mug. Pour boiling water over the mixture. Stir until the mix is completely dissolved. Package of Toffee Coffee Mix makes 5 to 8 servings.

A friend is one before whom I may think aloud.

-Ralph Waldo Emerson

- - - - - - - - - - - - - fold - - - - - - - - - - - - - -

Toffee Coffee

To make one serving:
2 to 3 tsp. Toffee Coffee Mix
8 ounces (1 cup) boiling water

Place the Toffee Coffee Mix in a mug. Pour boiling water over the mixture. Stir until the mix is completely dissolved. Package of Toffee Coffee Mix makes 5 to 8 servings.

Try not to become a person
of success but rather
a person of value.
-Albert Einstein

- - - - - - - - - - fold- - - - - - - - - - - - -

Chocolate Mint Coffee Mix

2 T. plus 2 tsp. sugar
2 T. instant coffee granules
2 T. powdered coffee creamer
2 tsp. unsweetened cocoa
1 peppermint candy, crushed into fine
pieces

Combine the above ingredients and stir until well blended. Place in a 3" x 4" ziplock bag and seal.

Attach a gift tag with the directions on how to prepare the coffee.

Chocolate Mint Coffee

To make one serving:
1 1/2 T. Chocolate Mint Coffee Mix
6 ounces (3/4 cup) boiling water
Whipped cream and candy cane, optional

Place the Chocolate Mint Coffee Mix in a mug. Pour boiling water over the mixture. Stir until the mix is completely dissolved. If desired, garnish with whipped cream and a candy cane. Package of Chocolate Mint Coffee Mix makes 5 to 8 servings.

Chocolate Mint Coffee

To make one serving:
1 1/2 T. Chocolate Mint Coffee Mix
6 ounces (3/4 cup) boiling water
Whipped cream and candy cane, optional

Place the Chocolate Mint Coffee Mix in a mug. Pour boiling water over the mixture. Stir until the mix is completely dissolved. If desired, garnish with whipped cream and a candy cane. Package of Chocolate Mint Coffee Mix makes 5 to 8 servings.

The best and most beautiful things in the world cannot be seen or even touched. They must be felt with the heart.

-Helen Keller

- - - - - - - fold - - - - - - - - - - - - -

Chocolate Mint Coffee

To make one serving:
1 1/2 T. Chocolate Mint Coffee Mix
6 ounces (3/4 cup) boiling water
Whipped cream and candy cane, optional

Place the Chocolate Mint Coffee Mix in a mug. Pour boiling water over the mixture. Stir until the mix is completely dissolved. If desired, garnish with whipped cream and a candy cane. Package of Chocolate Mint Coffee Mix makes 5 to 8 servings.

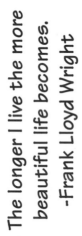

The longer I live the more
beautiful life becomes.
-Frank Lloyd Wright

 -fold-

Friendship Tea Mix

4 T. powdered orange flavored drink mix
2 T. presweetened lemonade mix
1 T. unsweetened instant tea
1 T. sugar
1/8 tsp. ground cloves
1/8 tsp. ground cinnamon

Combine the above ingredients and stir until well blended. Place in a 3" x 4" ziplock bag and seal.

Attach a gift tag with the directions on how to prepare the tea.

Friendship Tea

To make one serving:
2 tsp. Friendship Tea Mix
8 ounces (1 cup) boiling water
Cinnamon stick, optional

Place the Friendship Tea Mix in a mug. Pour boiling water over the mixture. Stir until the mix is completely dissolved. If desired, garnish with a cinnamon stick. Package of Friendship Tea Mix makes 12 servings.

Friendship Tea

To make one serving:
2 tsp. Friendship Tea Mix
8 ounces (1 cup) boiling water
Cinnamon stick, optional

Place the Friendship Tea Mix in a mug. Pour boiling water over the mixture. Stir until the mix is completely dissolved. If desired, garnish with a cinnamon stick. Package of Friendship Tea Mix makes 12 servings.

Like the honey to the bee
so are the cookies to the tea.

- - - - - fold - - - - -

Friendship Tea

To make one serving:
2 tsp. Friendship Tea Mix
8 ounces (1 cup) boiling water
Cinnamon stick, optional

Place the Friendship Tea Mix in a mug. Pour boiling water over the mixture. Stir until the mix is completely dissolved. If desired, garnish with a cinnamon stick. Package of Friendship Tea Mix makes 2 servings.

In youth we learn;
in age we understand.
-Marie von Ebner-Eschenbach

- - - - - - - - fold- - - - - - - -

Mocha Cappuccino Coffee Mix

1 T. powdered coffee creamer
1 T. unsweetened cocoa
2 1/2 T. sugar
1 T. instant coffee granules
1/2 tsp. ground cinnamon

Combine the above ingredients and stir until well blended. Place in a 3" x 4" ziplock bag and seal.

Attach a gift tag with the directions on how to prepare the coffee.

Mocha Cappuccino Coffee

To make one serving:
1 T. Mocha Cappuccino Coffee Mix
8 ounces (1 cup) boiling water
Whipped cream, optional

Place the Mocha Cappuccino Coffee Mix in a mug. Pour boiling water over the mixture. Stir until the mix is completely dissolved. If desired, garnish with whipped cream. Package of Mocha Cappuccino Coffee Mix makes 5 to 6 servings.

Mocha Cappuccino Coffee

To make one serving:
1 T. Mocha Cappuccino Coffee Mix
8 ounces (1 cup) boiling water
Whipped cream, optional

Place the Mocha Cappuccino Coffee Mix in a mug. Pour boiling water over the mixture. Stir unt'l the mix is completely dissolved. If desired, garnish with whipped cream. Package of Mocha Cappuccino Coffee Mix makes 5 to 6 servings.

In matters of style, swim with the current; in matters of principle, stand like a rock.

-Thomas Jefferson

- - - - - - - - - - - fold - - - - - - - - - - -

Mocha Cappuccino Coffee

To make one serving:
1 T. Mocha Cappuccino Coffee Mix
8 ounces (1 cup) boiling water
Whipped cream, optional

Place the Mocha Cappuccino Coffee Mix in a mug. Pour boiling water over the mixture. Stir until the mix is completely dissolved. If desired, garnish with whipped cream. Package of Mocha Cappuccino Coffee Mix makes 5 to 6 servings.

Cheerfulness and contentment are great beautifiers and are famous preservers of youthful looks.

-Charles Dickens

- - - - - - - - - - fold - - - - - - - - - - - -

Spiced Mocha Coffee Mix

2 T. unsweetened cocoa
2 T. powdered instant dry milk
1 T. plus 1 tsp. instant coffee granules
1/2 tsp. dried orange peel
1/4 tsp. ground cinnamon

Combine the above ingredients and stir until well blended. Place in a 3" x 4" ziplock bag and seal.

Attach a gift tag with the directions on how to prepare the coffee.

Spiced Mocha Coffee

To make one serving:
1 T. Spiced Mocha Coffee Mix
6 ounces (3/4 cup) boiling water
Shaved chocolate and cinnamon stick,
     optional

Place the Spiced Mocha Coffee Mix in a mug. Pour the boiling water over the mixture. Stir until the mix is completely dissolved. If desired, garnish with shaved chocolate and cinnamon stick. Package of Spiced Mocha Coffee Mix makes 5 to 6 servings.

Spiced Mocha Coffee

To make one serving:
1 T. Spiced Mocha Coffee Mix
6 ounces (3/4 cup) boiling water
Shaved chocolate and cinnamon stick, optional

Place the Spiced Mocha Coffee Mix in a mug. Pour the boiling water over the mixture. Stir until the mix is completely dissolved. If desired, garnish with shaved chocolate and cinnamon stick. Package of Spiced Mocha Coffee Mix makes 5 to 6 servings.

We make a living by what we get,
but we make a life by what we give.

-Winston Churchill

- - - - - - fold - - - - - - -

Spiced Mocha Coffee

To make one serving:

1 T. Spiced Mocha Coffee Mix
6 ounces (3/4 cup) boiling water
Shaved chocolate and cinnamon stick, optional

Place the Spiced Mocha Coffee Mix in a mug. Pour the boiling water over the mixture. Stir until the mix is completely dissolved. If desired, garnish with shaved chocolate and cinnamon stick. Package of Spiced Mocha Coffee Mix makes 5 to 6 servings.

I have but one lamp by which my feet are guided, and that is the lamp of experience. I know of no way of judging the future but by the past.

-Patrick Henry

Fireside Coffee Mix

1 T. plus 1 3/4 tsp. powdered coffee creamer
3 1/2 tsp. instant hot cocoa mix
3 1/2 tsp. instant coffee granules
1/8 tsp. ground cinnamon
1/8 tsp. ground nutmeg

Combine the above ingredients and stir until well blended. Place in a 3" x 4" ziplock bag and seal.

Attach a gift tag with the directions on how to prepare the coffee.

Fireside Coffee

To make one serving:
1 T. Fireside Coffee Mix
8 ounces (1 cup) boiling water

Place the Fireside Coffee Mix in a mug. Pour boiling water over the mixture. Stir until the mix is completely dissolved. Package of Fireside Coffee Mix makes 4 servings.

Fireside Coffee

To make one serving:
1 T. Fireside Coffee Mix
8 ounces (1 cup) boiling water

Place the Fireside Coffee Mix in a mug. Pour boiling water over the mixture. Stir until the mix is completely dissolved. Package of Fireside Coffee Mix makes 4 servings.

The pessimist sees the difficulty in every opportunity. The optimist, the opportunity in every difficulty.
-Winston Churchill

- - - - - - - - - - - - fold- - - - - - - - - - - - -

Fireside Coffee

To make one serving:
1 T. Fireside Coffee Mix
8 ounces (1 cup) boiling water

Place the Fireside Coffee Mix in a mug. Pour boiling water over the mixture. Stir until the mix is completely dissolved. Package of Fireside Coffee Mix makes 4 servings.

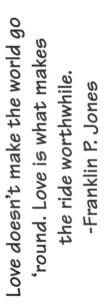

Love doesn't make the world go 'round. Love is what makes the ride worthwhile.

-Franklin P. Jones

- - - fold - - -

Chocolate Mint Hot Cocoa Mix

3 T. powdered instant dry milk
2 T. powdered chocolate flavored malted
   milk drink mix
1 1/2 T. instant hot cocoa mix
1 T. crushed butter mints

Combine the above ingredients and stir until well blended. Place in a 3" x 4" ziplock bag and seal.

Attach a gift card with the directions on how to prepare the hot cocoa.

Chocolate Mint Hot Cocoa

To make one serving:
4 T. Chocolate Mint Hot Cocoa Mix
6 ounces (3/4 cup) boiling water
Marshmallows and candy cane, optional

Place the Chocolate Mint Hot Cocoa Mix in a mug. Pour boiling water over the mixture. Stir until the mix is completely dissolved. If desired, garnish with marshmallows and candy cane. Package of Chocolate Mint Hot Cocoa Mix makes 2 servings.

Chocolate Mint Hot Cocoa

To make one serving:
4 T. Chocolate Mint Hot Cocoa Mix
6 ounces (3/4 cup) boiling water
Marshmallows and candy cane, optional

Place the Chocolate Mint Hot Cocoa Mix in a mug. Pour boiling water over the mixture. Stir until the mix is completely dissolved. If desired, garnish with marshmallows and candy cane. Package of Chocolate Mint Hot Cocoa Mix makes 2 servings.

Love at first sight is easy to understand. It's when two people have been looking at each other for years that it becomes a miracle.

-Sam Levinson

- - - - - - - - - - - fold - - - - - - - - - - -

Chocolate Mint Hot Cocoa

To make one serving:
4 T. Chocolate Mint Hot Cocoa Mix
6 ounces (3/4 cup) boiling water
Marshmallows and candy cane, optional

Place the Chocolate Mint Hot Cocoa Mix in a mug.
Pour boiling water over the mixture. Stir until the mix is
completely dissolved. If desired, garnish with marshmallows
and candy cane. Package of Chocolate Mint Hot Cocoa Mix
makes 2 servings.

Kind words can be short and easy
to speak, but their echoes are
truly endless.
-Mother Teresa

- fold-

Café Vienna Mix

2 T. plus 2 tsp. sugar
2 T. plus 2 tsp. powdered instant dry milk
2 T. instant coffee granules
1/8 tsp. ground cinnamon

Combine the above ingredients and stir until well blended. Place in a 3" x 4" ziplock bag and seal.

Attach a gift tag with the directions on how to prepare the coffee.

❀ Fill a gift basket with hot drink mixes, marshmallows, chocolate, one or two mugs and a book. ❀

Café Vienna

To make one serving:
2 to 2 1/2 tsp. Café Vienna Mix
8 ounces (1 cup) boiling water

Place the Café Vienna Mix in a mug. Pour boiling water over the mixture. Stir until the mix is completely dissolved. Package of Café Vienna Mix makes 8 to 11 servings.

Café Vienna

To make one serving:
2 to 2 1/2 tsp. Café Vienna Mix
8 ounces (1 cup) boiling water

Place the Café Vienna Mix in a mug. Pour boiling water over the mixture. Stir until the mix is completely dissolved. Package of Café Vienna Mix makes 8 to 11 servings.

Friends... they cherish each other's hopes. They are kind to each other's dreams.
-Henry David Thoreau

- fold -

Café Vienna

To make one serving:
2 to 2 1/2 tsp. Café Vienna Mix
8 ounces (1 cup) boiling water

Place the Café Vienna Mix in a mug. Pour boiling water over the mixture. Stir until the mix is completely dissolved. Package of Café Vienna Mix makes 8 to 11 servings.

You cannot do a kindness too
soon, for you never know how soon
it will be too late.
-Ralph Waldo Emerson

fold

Mulled Cider Mix

2 cinnamon sticks, broken in
    half if necessary
6 whole cloves
1 tsp. whole allspice
1/8 tsp. ground ginger

Combine the above ingredients and stir until well blended. Place in a 3" x 4" ziplock bag and seal.

Attach a gift tag with the directions on how to prepare the cider.

Mulled Cider

1 pkg. Mulled Cider Mix
1 quart apple cider
1/2 C. rum or brandy, optional

Heat the apple cider with the Mulled Cider Mix until the cider is hot. Do not allow the cider to boil. If desired, add 1/2 cup rum or brandy to the cider and heat through or add 1 tablespoon rum or brandy to each mug of cider.

Mulled Cider

1 pkg. Mulled Cider Mix
1 quart apple cider
1/2 C. rum or brandy, optional

Heat the apple cider with the Mulled Cider Mix until the cider is hot. Do not allow the cider to boil. If desired, add 1/2 cup rum or brandy to the cider and heat through or add 1 tablespoon rum or brandy to each mug of cider.

Never underestimate the power of simple courtesy. Your courtesy may not be returned or remembered, but discourtesy will.

-Princess Jackson Smith

- - - - - - - - - - -fold- - - - - - - - - - -

Mulled Cider

1 pkg. Mulled Cider Mix
1 quart apple cider
1/2 C. rum or brandy, optional

Heat the apple cider with the Mulled Cider Mix until the cider is hot. Do not allow the cider to boil. If desired, add 1/2 cup rum or brandy to the cider and heat through or add 1 tablespoon rum or brandy to each mug of cider.

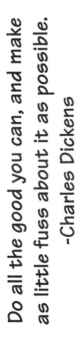

Do all the good you can, and make
as little fuss about it as possible.

-Charles Dickens

- - - - - - - - - - - - fold- - - - - - - - - - - -

Spiced Lemon Tea Mix

4 1/2 T. sugar
4 T. lemon flavored instant tea
1/4 tsp. plus 1/8 tsp. ground ginger
1/4 tsp. ground allspice

Combine the above ingredients and stir until well blended. Place in a 3" x 4" ziplock bag and seal.

Attach a gift tag with the directions on how to prepare the tea.

Spiced Lemon Tea

To make one serving:
1 1/2 to 2 T. Spiced Lemon Tea Mix
8 ounces (1 cup) boiling water

Place the Spiced Lemon Tea Mix in a mug. Pour boiling water over the mixture. Stir until the mix is completely dissolved. Package of Spiced Lemon Tea Mix makes 4 to 5 servings.

Spiced Lemon Tea

To make one serving:
1 1/2 to 2 T. Spiced Lemon Tea Mix
8 ounces (1 cup) boiling water

Place the Spiced Lemon Tea Mix in a mug. Pour boiling water over the mixture. Stir until the mix is completely dissolved. Package of Spiced Lemon Tea Mix makes 4 to 5 servings.

Never lose a chance of
saying a kind word.
-William Thackeray

- - - - - - - - - - - fold - - - - - - - - - - -

Spiced Lemon Tea

To make one serving:
1 1/2 to 2 T. Spiced Lemon Tea Mix
8 ounces (1 cup) boiling water

Place the Spiced Lemon Tea Mix in a mug. Pour boiling water over the mixture. Stir until the mix is completely dissolved. Package of Spiced Lemon Tea Mix makes 4 to 5 servings.

Even much worse than a storm or a riot, is a bunch of kids who are suddenly quiet.

- - - - - - - - fold - - - - - - - - -

Cinnamon Cappuccino Mix

5 1/2 tsp. sugar
1 T. powdered coffee creamer
1 T. powdered sugar
2 tsp. instant coffee granules
1/4 tsp. ground cinnamon

Combine the above ingredients and stir until well blended. Place in a 3" x 4" ziplock bag and seal.

Attach a gift tag with the directions on how to prepare the cappuccino.

Cinnamon Cappuccino

To make one serving:
1 1/2 to 2 T. Cinnamon Cappuccino Mix
8 ounces (1 cup) boiling water
Whipped cream and shaved chocolate,
optional

Place the Cinnamon Cappuccino Mix in a mug. Pour boiling water over the mixture. Stir until the mix is completely dissolved. If desired, garnish with whipped cream and shaved chocolate. Package of Cinnamon Cappuccino Mix makes 2 to 3 servings.

Cinnamon Cappuccino

To make one serving:

1 1/2 to 2 T. Cinnamon Cappuccino Mix
8 ounces (1 cup) boiling water
Whipped cream and shaved chocolate, optional

Place the Cinnamon Cappuccino Mix in a mug. Pour boiling water over the mixture. Stir until the mix is completely dissolved. If desired, garnish with whipped cream and shaved chocolate. Package of Cinnamon Cappuccino Mix makes 2 to 3 servings.

A candle loses nothing by lighting another candle.

- - - - - - - - - - fold - - - - - - - - - -

Cinnamon Cappuccino

To make one serving:

1 1/2 to 2 T. Cinnamon Cappuccino Mix
8 ounces (1 cup) boiling water
Whipped cream and shaved chocolate, optional

Place the Cinnamon Cappuccino Mix in a mug. Pour boiling water over the mixture. Stir until the mix is completely dissolved. If desired, garnish with whipped cream and shaved chocolate. Package of Cinnamon Cappuccino Mix makes 2 to 3 servings.

Love looks not with the eyes, but
with the heart.
-William Shakespeare

- - - - - - - - - fold - - - - - - - - -

Nightcap Coffee Mix

2 T. plus 2 tsp. instant coffee creamer
1 T. plus 1 tsp. instant coffee granules
1 T. plus 1 tsp. sugar
1/8 tsp. ground cardamom
1/8 tsp. ground cinnamon

Combine the above ingredients and stir until well blended. Place in a 3" x 4" ziplock bag and seal.

Attach a gift tag with the directions on how to prepare the coffee.

Nightcap Coffee

To make one serving:
1 heaping T. Nightcap Coffee Mix
8 ounces (1 cup) boiling water

Place the Nightcap Coffee Mix in a mug. Pour boiling water over the mixture. Stir until the mix is completely dissolved. Package of Nightcap Coffee Mix makes 4 to 5 servings.

Nightcap Coffee

To make one serving:
1 heaping T. Nightcap Coffee Mix
8 ounces (1 cup) boiling water

Place the Nightcap Coffee Mix in a mug. Pour boiling water over the mixture. Stir until the mix is completely dissolved. Package of Nightcap Coffee Mix makes 4 to 5 servings.

The only true gift is a
portion of thyself.
-Ralph Waldo Emerson

fold

Nightcap Coffee

To make one serving:
1 heaping T. Nightcap Coffee Mix
8 ounces (1 cup) boiling water

Place the Nightcap Coffee Mix in a mug. Pour boiling water over the mixture. Stir until the mix is completely dissolved. Package of Nightcap Coffee Mix makes 4 to 5 servings.

Be great in little things.
-St. Francis Xavier

- - - - - - - - - - fold - - - - - - - - - -

French Silk Mocha Mix

4 tsp. instant coffee granules
1 1/8 tsp. unsweetened cocoa
2 T. plus 2 tsp. sugar
2 T. powdered coffee creamer
1 1/2 tsp. powdered instant dry milk

Combine the above ingredients and stir until well blended. Place in a 3" x 4" ziplock bag and seal.

Attach a gift tag with the directions on how to prepare the mocha.

French Silk Mocha

To make one serving:
2 1/2 to 3 tsp. French Silk Mocha Mix
8 ounces (1 cup) boiling water
Whipped cream and shaved chocolate, optional

Place the French Silk Mocha Mix in a mug. Pour boiling water over the mixture. Stir until the mix is completely dissolved. If desired, garnish with whipped cream and shaved chocolate. Package of French Silk Mocha Mix makes 4 to 5 servings.

French Silk Mocha

To make one serving:
2 1/2 to 3 tsp. French Silk Mocha Mix
8 ounces (1 cup) boiling water
Whipped cream and shaved chocolate, optional

Place the French Silk Mocha Mix in a mug. Pour boiling water over the mixture. Stir until the mix is completely dissolved. If desired, garnish with whipped cream and shaved chocolate. Package of French Silk Mocha Mix makes 4 to 5 servings.

Gratitude is the heart's memory.

- - - - - fold- - - - -

French Silk Mocha

To make one serving:

2 1/2 to 3 tsp. French Silk Mocha Mix
8 ounces (1 cup) boiling water
Whipped cream and shaved chocolate, optional

Place the French Silk Mocha Mix in a mug. Pour boiling water over the mixture. Stir until the mix is completely dissolved. If desired, garnish with whipped cream and shaved chocolate. Package of French Silk Mocha Mix makes 4 to 5 servings.

Have a heart that never hardens, a temper that never tries, and a touch that never hurts.

-Charles Dickens

- - - - - - - - - fold- - - - - - - - -

Chocolate Coffee Mix

3 T. powdered coffee creamer
1 T. instant coffee granules
1 T. powdered chocolate flavored drink mix
1 1/2 tsp. sugar
Dash ground cinnamon

Combine the above ingredients and stir until well blended. Place in a 3" x 4" ziplock bag and seal.

Attach a gift tag with the directions on how to prepare the coffee.

Chocolate Coffee

To make one serving:
2 to 2 1/2 tsp. Chocolate Coffee Mix
8 ounces (1 cup) boiling water

Place the Chocolate Coffee Mix in a mug. Pour boiling water over the mixture. Stir until the mix is completely dissolved. Package of Chocolate Coffee Mix makes 5 to 6 servings.

Chocolate Coffee

To make one serving:

2 to 2 1/2 tsp. Chocolate Coffee Mix

8 ounces (1 cup) boiling water

Place the Chocolate Coffee Mix in a mug. Pour boiling water over the mixture. Stir until the mix is completely dissolved. Package of Chocolate Coffee Mix makes 5 to 6 servings.

Kind words can be short and easy
to speak, but their echoes
are truly endless.
-Mother Teresa

- - - - fold - - - - -

Chocolate Coffee

To make one serving:
2 to 2 1/2 tsp. Chocolate Coffee Mix
8 ounces (1 cup) boiling water

Place the Chocolate Coffee Mix in a mug. Pour boiling water over the mixture. Stir until the mix is completely dissolved. Package of Chocolate Coffee Mix makes 5 to 6 servings.

Well done is better than well said.

-Benjamin Franklin

- - - - - - - - - - - - - - fold - - - - - - - - - - - - - -

Cappuccino Mix

4 T. powdered chocolate flavored drink mix
3 T. powdered coffee creamer
2 T. instant coffee granules
1/8 tsp. ground cinnamon
1/8 tsp. ground nutmeg

Combine the above ingredients and stir until well blended. Place in a 3" x 4" ziplock bag and seal.

Attach a gift tag with the directions on how to prepare the cappuccino.

Cappuccino

To make one serving:
1 heaping T. Cappuccino Mix
8 ounces (1 cup) boiling water
Whipped cream and shaved chocolate, optional

Place the Cappuccino Mix in a mug. Pour boiling water over the mixture. Stir until the mix is completely dissolved. If desired, garnish with whipped cream and shaved chocolate. Package of Cappuccino Mix makes 7 to 8 servings.

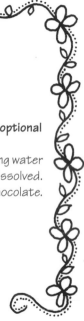

Cappuccino

To make one serving:

1 heaping T. Cappuccino Mix
8 ounces (1 cup) boiling water
Whipped cream and shaved chocolate, optional

Place the Cappuccino Mix in a mug. Pour boiling water over the mixture. Stir until the mix is completely dissolved. If desired, garnish with whipped cream and shaved chocolate. Package of Cappuccino Mix makes 7 to 8 servings.

Honesty is the first chapter
in the book of wisdom.
-Thomas Jefferson

- - - - - - - - - - fold - - - - - - - - - -

Cappuccino

To make one serving:

1 heaping T. Cappuccino Mix
8 ounces (1 cup) boiling water
Whipped cream and shaved chocolate, optional

Place the Cappuccino Mix in a mug. Pour boiling water over the mixture. Stir until the mix is completely dissolved. If desired, garnish with whipped cream and shaved chocolate. Package of Cappuccino Mix makes 7 to 8 servings.

Love doesn't make the world go 'round. Love is what makes the ride worthwhile.

-Franklin P. Jones

- - - - - - - - - - - -fold- - - - - - - - - - - -

French Vanilla Cappuccino Mix

2 T. plus 2 tsp. sugar
2 T. plus 2 tsp. French Vanilla flavored
    powdered coffee creamer
1 T. plus 1 tsp. powdered instant dry milk
1 T. plus 1 tsp. instant coffee granules

Combine the above Ingredients and stir until well blended. Place in a 3" x 4" ziplock bag and seal.

Attach a gift tag with the directions on how to prepare the cappuccino.

French Vanilla Cappuccino

To make one serving:
1 heaping T. French Vanilla Cappuccino Mix
8 ounces (1 cup) boiling water
Whipped cream and shaved chocolate, optional

Place the French Vanilla Cappuccino Mix in a mug. Pour boiling water over the mixture. Stir until the mix is completely dissolved. If desired, garnish with whipped cream and shaved chocolate. Package of French Vanilla Cappuccino Mix makes 7 to 8 servings.

French Vanilla Cappuccino

To make one serving:

1 heaping T. French Vanilla Cappuccino Mix
8 ounces (1 cup) boiling water
Whipped cream and shaved chocolate, optional

Place the French Vanilla Cappuccino Mix in a mug. Pour boiling water over the mixture. Stir until the mix is completely dissolved. If desired, garnish with whipped cream and shaved chocolate. Package of French Vanilla Cappuccino Mix makes 7 to 8 servings.

The best way to cheer yourself
up is to try to cheer
somebody else up.
-Mark Twain

- fold -

French Vanilla Cappuccino

To make one serving:
1 heaping T. French Vanilla Cappuccino Mix
8 ounces (1 cup) boiling water
Whipped cream and shaved chocolate, optional

Place the French Vanilla Cappuccino Mix in a mug. Pour boiling water over the mixture. Stir until the mix is completely dissolved. If desired, garnish with whipped cream and shaved chocolate. Package of French Vanilla Cappuccino Mix makes 7 to 8 servings.

Whether you think that you can,
or that you can't, you
are usually right.
-Henry Ford

- fold- - - - - - -

Peppermint Hot Chocolate Mix

> 2 T. powdered instant dry milk
> 2 T. powdered coffee creamer
> 2 T. sugar
> 1 T. unsweetened cocoa
> 1 peppermint candy, crushed into
>   fine pieces

Combine the above ingredients and stir until well blended. Place in a 3" x 4" ziploc bag and seal.

Attach a gift tag with the directions on how to prepare the hot chocolate.

Peppermint Hot Chocolate

To make one serving:
1 1/2 to 2 T. Peppermint Hot Chocolate Mix
6 ounces (3/4 cup) boiling water
Whipped cream and candy cane, optional

Place the Peppermint Hot Chocolate Mix in a mug. Pour boiling water over the mixture. Stir until the mix is completely dissolved. If desired, garnish with whipped cream and candy cane. Package of Peppermint Hot Chocolate Mix makes 3 to 4 servings.

Peppermint Hot Chocolate

To make one serving:

1 1/2 to 2 T. Peppermint Hot Chocolate Mix
6 ounces (3/4 cup) boiling water
Whipped cream and candy cane, optional

Place the Peppermint Hot Chocolate Mix in a mug. Pour boiling water over the mixture. Stir until the mix is completely dissolved. If desired, garnish with whipped cream and candy cane. Package of Peppermint Hot Chocolate Mix makes 3 to 4 servings.

A pint of example is worth
a gallon of advice.

- - - - - - fold - - - - - -

Peppermint Hot Chocolate

To make one serving:

1 1/2 to 2 T. Peppermint Hot Chocolate Mix
6 ounces (3/4 cup) boiling water
Whipped cream and candy cane, optional

Place the Peppermint Hot Chocolate Mix in a mug. Pour boiling water over the mixture. Stir until the mix is completely dissolved. If desired, garnish with whipped cream and candy cane. Package of Peppermint Hot Chocolate Mix makes 3 to 4 servings.

Happiness is not something you find, it's something you make.

- - - - - fold - - - - -

Russian Tea Mix

2 T. unsweetened instant tea
2 T. presweetened lemonade mix
2 T. powdered orange flavored drink mix
Dash ground cinnamon

Combine the above ingredients and stir until well blended. Place in a 3" x 4" ziplock bag and seal.

Attach a gift tag with the directions on how to prepare the tea.

Russian Tea

To make one serving:
2 tsp. Russian Tea Mix
8 ounces (1 cup) boiling water

Place the Russian Tea Mix in a mug. Pour boiling water over the mixture. Stir until the mix is completely dissolved. Package of Russian Tea Mix makes 7 to 10 servings.

Russian Tea

To make one serving:
2 tsp. Russian Tea Mix
8 ounces (1 cup) boiling water

Place the Russian Tea Mix in a mug. Pour boiling water over the mixture. Stir until the mix is completely dissolved. Package of Russian Tea Mix makes 7 to 10 servings.

Like the honey to the bee
so are the cookies to the tea.

- - - - - - - fold - - - - - - - - -

Russian Tea

To make one serving:
2 tsp. Russian Tea Mix
8 ounces (1 cup) boiling water

Place the Russian Tea Mix in a mug. Pour boiling water over the mixture. Stir until the mix is completely dissolved. Package of Russian Tea Mix makes 7 to 10 servings.

The secret of contentment
is knowing how to enjoy
what you have.

- - - - - - - - fold - - - - - - - -